Copyright 2000
All rights reserved. Published by Mindfull Publishing.

Photo credits: Front cover - U.S. Fish and Wildlife Service, back cover - Jack H. Hecht/LMS, title page and acknowledgement pages - U.S. Fish and Wildlife Service, egg to chick sequence - Scott Wright (4 week old chick by Jack H. Hecht/LMS), cutout bird on DDT page - Paul J. Fusco/CT DEP-Wildlife, Millennium Falcon courtesy of Lucasfilm Ltd.

Publisher's Cataloging-in-publication
(*Provided by Quality Books, Inc*)

Priebe, Mac
Wildlife winners : the peregrine falcon--endangered no more / by Mac Priebe ; illustrated by Jennifer Priebe. 1st ed.
p. cm.
SUMMARY: Tells how the peregrine falcon faced extinction, but has now been removed from the Endangered Species List because many groups worked to rebuild its population in North America.
LCCN: 98-74803
ISBN: 0-9669551-9-6

1. Peregrine falcon--Juvenile literature. 2. Birds, Protection of--Juvenile literature.
3. Endangered species--Law and legislation-- Juvenile literature.
I. Priebe, Jennifer. II. Title.
QL696.F34P75 1999
598.9'6   QBI99-98

First edition.

Wildlife Winners
The Peregrine Falcon
Endangered No More

by Mac Priebe
With Illustrations by Jennifer Priebe
Mindfull Publishing
Norwalk, Connecticut

If you could use a time machine to visit North America 20,000 years ago, you'd find some interesting animals. Saber-toothed cats and American mastodons flourished at that time. Nowadays, you'd be hard pressed to run across either, since they are **extinct** – there are no more living saber-toothed cats or American mastodons.

If you used the same time machine to go back 100 million years, you would find that dinosaurs roamed the Earth, similar to the way humans are the most noticeable **species** on the planet today. No matter where you traveled, you would probably run across a dinosaur. However, they are also extinct. We can only imagine what it might be like to cross the path of a great dinosaur.

Extinction

Why do species become extinct?   The answer usually depends on which species you're talking about. No one really knows what happened to the dinosaurs, although there is some agreement that the Earth's **environment** drastically changed around the time that they became extinct. It may be that the environment changed in a way that made it impossible for the dinosaur to survive.

In modern times, it is easy to see that humans have changed the environment. Where there used to be forests and jungles, there are now cities and roads. Humans burn a lot of fuels and use a lot of chemicals, which can change the air, land and water. With these environmental changes, it is possible that we make life more difficult for other animals. In fact, this has happened with several animals, and we're about to find out about one bird – the peregrine falcon – whose life has been seriously affected by the presence of humans in North America.

U.S. Fish and Wildlife Service

Falcon Fact

By the 1960's, peregrine falcons were disappearing all over North America. In fact, they were thought to be extinct east of the Mississippi River.

America's Most Endangered

Scientific name	Falco Peregrinus
Average weight	Female: about 2 pounds (900 grams) Male: about 1.5 pounds (675 grams)
Average length	Female: about 20 inches (50 cms) Male: about 15 inches (38 cms)
Style of nesting	On cliff ledges and buildings, 3-5 eggs.
Geographical distribution	Found worldwide; in North America, found from the Arctic Circle south into Central America.
Flight speed	Up to 200 miles per hour (320 km/h)
Diet	Smaller birds, occasional bats
Listed as endangered	1970

The Peregrine Falcon

The peregrine falcon belongs to a group of birds known as **"raptors"**. This falcon is found throughout the United States, Canada, and all over the world.

The peregrine likes to nest on ledges. Because they like high places, they have learned to nest on tall buildings in cities as well. Since they hunt smaller birds, and cities are usually full of birds (such as pigeons and sparrows), it makes sense that peregrine falcons would feel at home in the city.

The peregrine falcon is a **predator** that hunts for its food. The falcon's **prey** consists of smaller birds which are caught while flying. To do this, the peregrine uses its keen eyesight, its terrific speed, its grasping talons and hooked beak. The falcon can fly faster than any bird on Earth. In fact, it is believed to be the fastest of any creature in the world. Some people have nicknamed the peregrine "Sky Ripper".

This falcon lives on the Bank of New York building in New York City. It is about 35 stories up.

Species in Danger

In the 1960s, scientists noticed that a lot of peregrine falcons in North America were disappearing. The population of peregrines had fallen from several thousand to just a few hundred. In fact, the falcon had completely disappeared from the eastern United States and the Canadian maritime provinces. Only a half dozen peregrine falcons were known to exist in Alberta, Canada. Scientists were alarmed by this decline in population and began searching for the reason.

It turned out that many peregrine falcons had a large amount of a chemical called "**DDT**" in their bodies. DDT is a chemical that farmers sprayed on their crops to keep insects away.

Falcon Fact

By the early 1970s, the Canadian and U.S. governments had passed laws to protect endangered species. They also made the use of the poison, DDT, illegal.

POISON

What does DDT do?

DDT can cause problems in two ways. DDT is poisonous if enough of it gets into the body. Therefore, a falcon can die if it takes in enough DDT. However, it is not known whether this actually happens to the peregrine falcon.

The second way DDT can cause problems is if it interrupts the production of eggs and the **hatching** of falcon chicks; if no new falcons are hatched, then the population will eventually disappear. In fact, scientists believe that this is the most important effect that DDT has had on the peregrine falcon.

DDT prevents a nutrient called "calcium" from being used in the making of eggshells. So, while the mother is producing the eggs, calcium is not getting into the shells. Since the eggshells lack calcium, they are weak and crumble easily. Therefore, when the mother sits on the eggs to keep them warm, she often crushes them. If the eggs are crushed before the chicks hatch, there will be no new peregrine falcons. This is what was happening to the peregrine falcons in North America.

DDT and the Food Chain

Peregrine falcons accumulated large amounts of DDT because of a scientific process called **biological magnification**. This process affects animals at the top of the **food chain** the most, and the peregrine falcon is at the top of its food chain. Here's how it works:

Let's say an insect lands on a cornstalk that has been dusted with DDT. A certain amount of the DDT gets into the insect. One of the reasons that DDT was used against insects was because it is not removed from the body once it gets in – it stays there until the animal dies. Now, if a larger insect eats that insect before it dies from DDT poisoning, the larger insect also eats all the DDT, which then stays in the larger insect until it dies. And if the larger insect eats several poisoned insects, it accumulates more and more DDT.

Now let's say a small bird eats our larger insect. Once again, it accumulates all of that DDT (which was never removed from the body). And if it eats several insects, the amount of DDT in its body rises higher and higher. Finally, let's say the peregrine falcon eats a lot of these small birds – it will also acquire all the DDT that each smaller bird had gotten from eating a lot of poisoned insects. At each level of the food chain, DDT was magnified to a higher concentration – thus, the process is called biological magnification. As a result of this, DDT became very concentrated at the top of the food chain – which was bad news for the peregrine falcon.

Governments Spring into Action

Once scientists realized that the peregrine falcon was disappearing, it was not long before people began to take measures to save it. In 1970, the peregrine was officially declared an endangered species.

The U.S. government has a law called the "Endangered Species Act" which defines what makes a species in danger of extinction and how to deal with it. Firstly, animals of an endangered species are not allowed to be hunted, killed, wounded, captured or taken as a pet. The animal is to be left alone by the public. Along the same lines, the Act calls for the **habitat** of the peregrine also to receive protection. Hence, it would be illegal to destroy any area that peregrines need to survive.

The Act calls for the design of a recovery strategy; an attempt is to be made

to help the species return to a thriving state. Since it is not an easy task to assist a species in recovery, the Act requires an organized plan of action be constructed.   The Canadian government also created its own recovery plan, known as the Anatum   Peregrine Falcon Recovery Plan.

In 1970, Canada outlawed the use of DDT, and the

Jack Hecht LM

U.S. government did the same two years later. Outlawing DDT was probably the most important step in saving the peregrine falcon, but without the help of humans all over North America, the recovery of the falcons may not have occurred.

Falcon Fact

The female falcon stays on the nest to care for her chicks. The male hunts and brings back food for his family.

Day 1

A Plan of Action

It would seem simple enough to say that the peregrine falcon recovery would be successful once the number of falcons in North America reached a certain number. While this is very important, the government's plan also established a list of several goals for healthy peregrine life. First, North America was divided into 5 regions (Alaska, Canada, the Eastern United States, Rocky Mountains / American Southwest, and along the coast of the Pacific Ocean), and a population goal was set for each region. Second, mating pairs were to reach a goal for raising young successfully – if the number of falcons was

high, but none of the falcons could raise chicks, it wouldn't be long before the species was in danger again. Thirdly, the average amount of DDT in the population must significantly decrease to a certain level. Lastly, eggshells needed to return to a more normal thickness.

Falcon Fact

One of the most famous and intelligent dinosaurs was the velociraptor, which is referred to as the "Raptor" for short. However, the word "raptor" refers to a group of predatory birds who use their sharp **talons** to hold on to their prey when hunting. In fact, "raptor" has been taken from a Latin word which means "to grasp".

On top of a skyscraper

1 week old

Starting From Scratch

Since there were so few peregrine falcons, and many of them were laying weak eggs, a helping hand was necessary to start the falcon on the road to recovery. The eggs would probably be crushed if the parents did the **incubating**. So, scientists set out to save the eggs from the few falcons that remained in the wild. This was not an easy task.

First of all, it is often difficult to take eggs from a bird's nest. Since the eggs are their future chicks, the parents defend them furiously. The peregrine falcon is no

The Millennium Falcon

Falcon Fact

Because of its speed, its keen senses, its power and its majestic bearing, the falcon has been chosen as the namesake for school and professional teams, as well as a famous spaceship.

exception. Also, the task was complicated by the fact that peregrine falcons nest on cliffs. So, mountain climbers had to scale these cliffs just to get to the nests.

After the eggs were taken, they were brought to a laboratory to be incubated. If the shells were already cracked, the scientists glued the shells back together. Some fragile eggs were coated with wax to protect them from losing moisture. The eggs had to be kept warm and rotated the same way they would have been if they were in the nest with their parents. After about a month, the falcon chicks were ready to hatch.

2 weeks old

New Life

A peregrine falcon chick is called an **eyas**. Once an eyas begins to hatch, it can take anywhere from 24 to 48 hours for it to completely emerge from the egg. Scientists would help weak chicks if they were having trouble hatching. The chick pecks in a circular motion until it finally pops out. Once hatched, the new eyas needs 8 to 12 hours of rest before it is ready for its first meal. In the lab, the chick was fed small chunks of meat for its first meal – just like it would be in the wild.

Humans cannot handle the eyas after it has opened its eyes. If they do, the falcon will grow up thinking that it is human. This behavior is called **imprinting**. However, the chicks still needed to be fed, so scientists used falcon puppets to feed the young birds.

After a few days, the chicks were placed in the nest of a tamed falcon that acted as a foster parent. After a few weeks, the young falcons were returned to their original parents in the wild.

Falcon Fact

Since the early 1970s, when people began to try to save the falcon from extinction, more than 6,000 falcon chicks have been helped to hatch and grow to healthy **fledglings.**

However, before they were released, scientists attached small identification bands to the birds' legs. By making use of the bands, scientists can keep track of where the falcons go and what they do.

At first, the chicks are covered with white **down**. When the young falcons are 6 weeks old, they start to look and act more and more like an adult. They learn how to fly, and soon after, they also learn how to hunt. The first feathers, which are brown, sprout around that time. At two years of age, they get the full range of their adult feathers.

Craig Koppie

3 weeks old

Hunting

The peregrine has a very impressive manner of hunting. Although the falcon normally flies at speeds around 60 miles per hour (100 km/h), it can reach speeds of around 200 mph (340 km/h) when hunting. This is because of a special flight technique. The peregrine flies high into the air and then draws its wings in towards its body as it begins its dive. By doing this, the falcon uses the Earth's gravity to accelerate – the falcon is basically falling faster and faster to Earth. Eventually, it reaches the victim and kills it by breaking its neck upon impact – the victim never knows what hits it and therefore does not suffer.

Falcon Fact

Female falcons are larger than males. The peregrine female is about one-third bigger than the male.

Peregrine Love

Soon, the young falcon's thoughts turn towards romance, and the process of choosing a mate will begin. Like humans, this is an important decision for a falcon; the partner chosen will be a partner for life. Therefore, the peregrine is said to be **monogamous** – it is faithful and loyal to one mating partner. Peregrine falcons may travel long distances before they finally find a mate. For example, there is a happy couple of peregrines living in Toronto who came a long way to meet one another – the male is from Williamsport, Pennsylvania, and the female is from Hamilton, Ontario.

Acts of kindness

Although a lot of work was done in the laboratory, every little bit of help outside the laboratory has been important, too. In Cleveland, a couple of falcons make their home on a skyscraper called the Terminal Tower, which is the main attraction in the city's skyline. Every 4th of July, there is an impressive fireworks display right by the building. This display could prove very dangerous to the falcons if one of them was struck by fallout from the fireworks. One year, a man used a small box to cover the chicks during the fireworks display, so that they wouldn't get hurt by any falling debris from the fireworks. Luckily, it was a cold night, so the young birds were huddled together to keep warm, making it easier to cover them. Another year, a couple of expecting parents were incubating some unhatched eggs in the nestbox. The Ohio Division of Wildlife kept an egg incu-bating machine nearby in case the fireworks scared away the parents and the eggs were left untended. That year, 50,000 people who were watching the fireworks sang "Rock-A-Bye Baby" to the young falcons.

Helping these birds may not always take a lot of effort, but, in their own way, many people have made important individual contributions to the recovery of the peregrine falcon.

4 weeks old

Nest box is on the 12th floor.

Falcon Fact

In nature, the falcon chooses a high place to nest, such as a cliff . It eats birds. The peregrine has **adapted** nicely to city life, living on skyscrapers and feasting on pigeons.

Number of Known Pairs in Each State

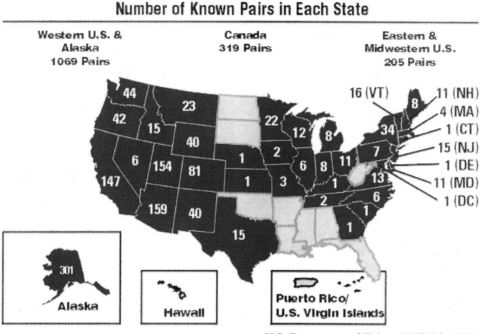

Western U.S. & Alaska 1069 Pairs	Canada 319 Pairs	Eastern & Midwestern U.S. 205 Pairs

16 (VT)
11 (NH)
4 (MA)
1 (CT)
15 (NJ)
1 (DE)
11 (MD)
1 (DC)

Alaska 301

Hawaii

Puerto Rico/ U.S. Virgin Islands

U.S. Department of Fish and Wildlife 1997

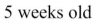

5 weeks old

Success

In August of 1998, the United States Fish and Wildlife Service officially proposed that the peregrine falcon be **de-listed**, or removed, from the Endangered Species List. In this proposal, the Service outlined the degree of success in each of the five regions in which a recovery effort was being made. The Service also asked for opinions about de-listing from the scientific community and the general public. In the proposal, the Service responds to all the issues raised by concerned Americans and assures us that de-listing will not place the peregrine at risk. However, people must continue to watch over and care for falcons, especially in cities. Scientists will continue to watch them carefully.

Recovery Goals and Accomplishments

Recovery Plan	Goal	Current Status	Comments
Alaska			
Mating pairs	28 pairs	301 pairs	Exceeded Goal
Number of young per pair	1.8 young / year	2.0 young / year	Exceeded Goal
DDT concentration	Under 5 ppm (parts per million)	3.5 ppm	Exceeded Goal
Eggshell thinning	Less than 10%	12.1%	Goal not met
Canada			
Mating pairs	60 pairs	319 pairs	Exceeded Goal
Number of young per pair	1.5 young / year	1.8 young / year	Exceeded Goal
Pacific Coast			
Mating pairs	185 pairs	301 pairs	Exceeded Goal
Number of young per pair	1.5 young / year	1.5 young / year	Goal met
Rocky Mountains / Southwest U.S.			
Mating pairs	183 pairs	301 pairs	Exceeded Goal
Number of young per pair	1.25 young / year	1.4 young / year	Exceeded Goal
Eggshell thinning	Less than 10%		Only measured in a few states
Eastern U.S.			
Mating pairs	200 pairs	174 pairs	Goal not reached, but there are 31 more pairs in midwestern states outside the recovery area.

U.S. Fish and Wildlife Service   1997

Mission Accomplished

And so this fight against extinction ends in victory as the peregrine falcon is removed from the federal Endangered Species List. All of the people who were involved in saving the falcon have every reason to feel proud; were it not for their efforts, North America might not have the peregrine falcon anymore. As we have learned, the falcon has had many helpers: scientists, lawmakers, concerned citizens, charity donors and many others have all made important contributions.

In an ideal world, the falcon would never have been in danger, and humans would not have used DDT in the first place. Although it was humans who caused the problem, it was also humans who came through for the falcon before it was too late. And after 30 years, and an extraordinary recovery effort, we can proudly and officially declare: the peregrine falcon is endangered no more.

6 week old fledgling -
ready to fly

Glossary

adapt - to change in structure, form or habits to fit different conditions

biological magnification - becoming more concentrated at each level of the food chain

de-listed - the term used when a species is removed from the federal Endangered Species List

DDT - a chemical used to kill unwanted insects

down - soft feathers of a bird

environment - the conditions, influences, and surroundings that affect any living thing

extinct - gone from the Earth, no longer existing

eyas - the name for a young falcon

fledgling - a young bird that has grown the feathers needed to fly and is old enough to take its first flight

food chain - the flow of energy from the sun to plants to animals

habitat - place where a plant or animal naturally grows or lives

hatch - to come out of an egg

imprinting - patterning behavior after the first creature a chick sees when it opens its eyes

incubate - to sit on eggs, or keep them warm, in order to hatch them

monogamous - having only one mate during a lifetime

predator - an animal that kills and eats other animals

prey - animal that is hunted and killed for food by another animal

raptor - a bird that kills other animals for food

species - level of classification of animals that may breed with one another

talon - claw of an animal, especially a bird of prey

Find Out About Falcons

Many states and provinces have information about wildlife. Contact your state or province department of fish and wildlife.

CANADA

The Canadian Peregrine Foundation
112 Merton St. Suite 300
Toronto, ON M4S2Z8
(416)481-1233
www.peregrine-foundation.ca

Environment Canada
4905 Duffin St.
Downsview,ON M3H5T4
www.ec,gc,ca

U. of Calgary Peregrine Falcon
Homepage
www.acs.ucalgary.ca/~tull/falcon

World Wildlife Fund Canada
245 Eglington Ave. E, Suite 410
Toronto, ON M4P3J6
(800)26-PANDA
(416)489-8800 in Toronto
www.wwfcanada.org

U.S.A.

Cleveland Peregrine Falcon Watch
www.CPFW.org

Hawk Mountain Sanctuary Assn.
1700 Hawk Mountain Rd.
Kempton, PA 19529
(610)756-6000
www.hawkmountain.org

U.S. Fish and Wildlife Service
www.fws.gov

Midwest Raptor Center
University of Minnesota
1920 Fitch Ave.
St. Paul, MN 55108
www.raptor.cvm.umn.edu

World Center for Birds of Prey
5666 Flying Hawk Lane
Boise, ID 83709
(208)362-3716
www.peregrinefund.org

Acknowledgements

Thank you to the falcon lovers who helped on this book. A special thanks to the World Center for Birds of Prey, the U.S. Fish and Wildlife Service-Division of Endangered Species, the New York Department of Environmental Conservation, the Connecticut Department of Environmental Protection, and Jack Hecht. Thank you, Scott Wright, Cleveland's own peregrine falcon watchdog. He is an example of all the concerned people across North America who have helped to restore the peregrine falcon to healthy numbers.